Take your camera to

GERMANY

Ted Park

www.raintreepublishers.co.uk
Visit our website to find out more information about Raintree books.

To order:
 Phone 44 (0) 1865 888112
 Send a fax to 44 (0) 1865 314091
 Visit the Raintree Bookshop at www.raintreepublishers.co.uk to browse
our catalogue and order online

First published in Great Britain by Raintree Publishers,
Halley Court, Jordan Hill, Oxford
OX2 8EJ, part of Harcourt Education.
Raintree is a registered trademark of Harcourt
Education Ltd.

© Harcourt Education Ltd 2003
First published in paperback in 2004
The moral right of the proprietor has been asserted.

Produced for Raintree by Discovery Books
Editors: Isabel Thomas and Gianna Williams
Cover design: Jo Sapwell (www.tipani.co.uk)

Printed and bound in China by South China
Printing Company

ISBN 1 844 21188 6 (hardback)
07 06 05 04 03
10 9 8 7 6 5 4 3 2 1

ISBN 1 844 21196 7 (paperback)
08 07 06 05 04
10 9 8 7 6 5 4 3 2 1

British Library cataloguing in Publication Data
Park, Ted
  Germany. – (Take Your Camera to)
  523.8

A full catalogue record for this book is available from
the British Library.

Acknowledgements
Cover photograph of the Brandenberg Gate
reproduced with permission of imagestate.

All statistics in the Quick Facts section come from
The New York Times Almanac (2002) and The World
Almanac (2002).

Every effort has been made to contact copyright
holders of any material reproduced in this book. Any
omissions will be rectified in subsequent printings if
notice is given to the publishers.

Contents

Any words appearing in the text in bold, **like this**, are explained in the glossary.

This is Germany

Germany is a country in the centre of Europe, full of mountains, forests, flat lands and gentle hills. There are beaches in the north, and mountains for skiing in the south.

The German countryside is dotted with ancient churches, **cathedrals** and castles. The Black Forest is in the south and is one of Germany's most famous regions. Take a boat ride down the River **Rhine**. The river's valley has beautiful little towns and bridges that would make great pictures.

Germany has five large cities: Berlin, Hamburg, **Munich**, Cologne and Frankfurt. Berlin is the largest city and the capital. Germany's main seaport is in Hamburg. Munich is the capital of the **Bavarian** region, Cologne is famous for its cathedral and Frankfurt is the financial centre of Germany.

The famous Cathedral of Cologne overlooks the River Rhine. Construction of the cathedral started in 1248 but it was not completed until 1880.

This book will show you some of the best things to see in Germany. You will learn interesting things about the country and the people who live there. So, when you're ready to take your camera there, you'll know exactly what to do and where to go.

The place

Germany is about 840 kilometres (520 miles) from north to south and about 620 kilometres (385 miles) from east to west. Germany has 356,910 square kilometres (137,803 square miles) of land within its borders. This means Germany is about three times the size of England.

Germany shares its borders with many other countries. Denmark, the Baltic sea and the North Sea border Germany in the north. France, Belgium, the Netherlands and Luxembourg border Germany to the west, and Poland and the Czech Republic are to the east. Switzerland and Austria border Germany to the south.

Denmark is a peninsula that extends from northern Germany. A peninsula is a piece of land that has water on three sides. Germany has its main seaports on the North Sea. The Baltic Sea has islands and beaches where people go on holiday.

Germany

- —— International Boundary
- ★ National Capital
- • Major Cities
- —— Rivers

0   50   100 Kilometres
0   50   100 Miles

DENMARK

Baltic Sea

North Sea

N
W E
S

NETHERLANDS
★ Amsterdam

Elbe

Oder

Warta

Berlin ★ POLAND

Weser

Oder

Rhine

GERMANY

Elbe

Neisse

•Dusseldorf

★ Brussels
BELGIUM

Cologne •
• Bonn

Werra

Frankfurt •

Main

Prague ★

CZECH
REPUBLIC

Rhein-Main-
Donau-Kanal

LUX.
★ Luxembourg

Rhine

• Heidelberg

BAVARIA

Danube

FRANCE

BLACK FOREST

AUSTRIA

SWITZERLAND

BAVARIAN ALPS
Zugspitze 9,720 ft.

7

People take tours along the River Rhine to see its beautiful buildings.

The country is hilly in the western and central parts. Southern Germany has snowy mountains and thick forests. The further south you travel, the higher the mountains get. These tall mountains are known as the **Bavarian** Alps. At 2963 metres high, the Zugspitze is Germany's highest alpine peak.

Germany has many rivers. The most famous river is the **Rhine**. Others include the Elbe, Weser, Ems and Main. Most of Germany's rivers are used to transport things the German people need or things they sell to others.

Western Germany generally has moderate or mild weather. This means it is usually never too hot or too cold. Even in the highest mountains of the south-west, warm winds keep the weather mild. Eastern Germany has a more extreme climate, with cold winters and short, hot summers.

Bavaria, located in Germany's southern region, has many rich, green forests and snowy mountains.

Berlin

Four years after World War Two ended, Germany was divided into two countries: East Germany and West Germany. The capital of West Germany was Bonn. The city of Berlin was also divided into two cities, East and West. East Berlin and East Germany were ruled by a **communist** government, while West Germany and West Berlin were **democratic**. West Berlin was surrounded by East Germany and became a small island of freedom where people could escape communism.

In 1961, the Berlin Wall was built to keep East Germans from escaping to West Berlin. The Berlin Wall was taken down in 1989 and Germany was made into one country again. Then the capital was moved from Bonn back to Berlin. During the 1990s, much of Berlin was rebuilt. The **Reichstag** or **parliament** building was rebuilt and became the centre of Germany's government again.

There are museums, palaces and historic buildings on the same street as the famous Brandenburg Gate.

Today Berlin is a new and exciting place. The **Brandenburg Gate** is one of Berlin's most famous sights. It is at the beginning of *Unter den Linden*, a wide, tree-lined street. If you visit Berlin, remember to take a picture of this beautiful building.

Places to visit

Germany's cities are as interesting to visit as the countryside. Hamburg is Germany's main seaport and second largest city. Streams and canals cross through the city. Canals are artificial waterways built to carry water traffic. Hamburg was bombed during World War Two and a lot of the city was destroyed. Today, much of it has been rebuilt. Although Hamburg is an **industrial** city, it also has some beautiful parks and gardens.

Munich is Germany's third largest city. Munich is the capital of the region of **Bavaria**. There is a famous palace in the middle of the city. This palace once belonged to the kings of Bavaria, but now it is a museum.

The **Rhine** Valley is one of Germany's most beautiful places. The river winds through the country from south to north. Nearby there are vineyards where grapes are grown and from the river you can see beautiful old castles.

This old castle has a great view of the Rhine Valley.

The people

More than 83 million people live in Germany. This makes Germany one of the most populated countries in Europe. About a third of all Germans live in cities, mainly in the western part.

Most Germans dress in everyday clothes, like jeans and T-shirts, or suits for work. But traditional dress is still worn in some place on special occasions. In the southern region of **Bavaria**, people sometimes wear *lederhosen*. Lederhosen are leather shorts with braces.

Germany did not become one country until 1871, so people are often more loyal to the region they live in than to the country. Many people in Bavaria, for example, still think of themselves as Bavarians first and Germans second.

Today, there are people in Germany who have come from other places looking for work. They are known as *gastarbeiter*, which means guest worker. These people came from eastern Europe, Italy and Turkey. Today,

This man wears a traditional costume while playing a tune on his accordion.

These people in Bavaria are wearing the traditional dress of that region.

almost one-tenth of the people living in Germany were born in another country.

High German is the language that developed in the regions of the south, but Germans speak differently in other parts of the country. These differences are known as dialects. A dialect is a different way of speaking the same language.

Life in Germany

Germans work hard but they have a lot of time to relax. Most Germans get four to six weeks' holiday each year. They like to travel and take part in outdoor activities. There are many **spa** towns in Germany, where people can bathe in the natural springs. In German, 'baden' means bath, so the spa towns have names like Wiesbaden or Baden-Baden.

Germans are book lovers and readers. In fact, after the USA, Germany has published the highest number of books. Germans also like to visit museums.

For breakfast, they have different types of meat, cheese and bread. Their biggest meal is at lunchtime with a lighter dinner in the evening. Germans like to eat out, too, and the big cities have good restaurants serving all kinds of German food as well as Chinese, Italian and Turkish dishes.

Many new and old buildings stand side by side in German cities.

Government and religion

Germany is made up of sixteen states, called *Länder*. The states are joined together into the **Federal Republic** of Germany. The German **parliament**, or **Reichstag**, makes the laws. It has two chambers, or branches. They are the Federal Assembly and the National Assembly. The head of the government is known as the chancellor. He or she is the leader of the party that has been elected to govern. Elect means to choose someone by voting. There is also a president, but that person has less power than the chancellor.

About a third of all Germans are **Protestants**. Most Protestants live in the north, and the majority of them belong to the Lutheran church. Germany was the home of Martin Luther. In the 16th century, he broke away from the Catholic Church and founded the Protestant religion.

While in Germany, don't forget to admire some of the fine, old government buildings.

Another third of all Germans are **Roman Catholics**. Most Catholics live in the southern part of the country. There are also about a million **Muslims** in Germany. Most German Muslims originally came from Turkey.

Earning a living

Germany is a country rich in **natural resources**, including coal and **iron ore**. Some people work as miners to bring them up out of the ground.

About a third of Germans work in **industry**. They are skilled at turning natural resources into products. In the north, making ships is an important industry and chemicals, steel, medicines, cars and cameras are among the largest German industries.

The motor car was invented in Germany in the 1870s. The car industry is Germany's biggest. Volkswagens were first built in Germany. It is also the home of the Mercedes Benz and BMW cars.

Germany is a rich country and during the 50 years that Germany was divided, the western part of the country developed quickly. But the eastern part fell behind. Today, there is still more unemployment and poverty in the east than in the west.

About half of the land in Germany is used for farming, but only a small number of people are farmers.

The car was invented in Germany in the 1870s. Skilled workers used to build the cars. Now, these robots do the job.

Germany's main seaports are on the North Sea coast.

Schools and sport

Most German children attend kindergarten between the ages of four and six. *Kindergarten* is a German word that means 'children's garden' in English. Then children go on to primary school from ages six to ten, after which they split into three categories: trade or vocational school, business schools or university preparatory schools. University preparatory schools usually take nine years to complete. In many areas, children have to go to school on Saturdays.

Germany has many universities and some of them have huge numbers of students. Germany's oldest university, at Heidelberg, was founded in 1386.

Germans like to spend time outdoors and enjoy skiing, camping, hiking and cycling. Football is the most popular team sport. Germans like to play football themselves and to watch their favourite teams play. Many places sponsor sports clubs. Some large German cities have

This German student is studying hard.

American-style football and basketball teams. German athletes often win a large share of the medals at the Olympic Games and some of the country's tennis players are world-beaters.

Food and Festivals

Germany is famous for its rich food. Many kinds of sausages, breads, potatoes, dumplings, **sauerkraut** and, of course, frankfurters are German staples. Desserts include cakes, gingerbread, strudel and stollen, a rich fruit cake.

Each year, in **Munich**, there is *Oktoberfest*. This is an autumn harvest festival, where food and drink, especially beer, are consumed in large amounts.

Many German cities have special markets in the weeks before Christmas. Shoppers can buy all kinds of food, decorations, toys and other gifts. Germans also celebrate Advent, the four weeks before Christmas. Advent calendars and Christmas trees come from Germany.

The idea of the Christmas tree came from Germany. If you go there during this time of year, don't forget your camera!

The 40-day period just before Easter is known as Lent. *Fasching*, or *Karneval* (the German word for 'Carnival'), comes just before Lent starts. It is a time for parties, parades and dressing up in costumes.

The future

If you took your camera to Germany, you would see a country that is changing quickly. Germany is at the centre of the European Union, a group of European countries that have joined together to improve trade and understanding. Germany has recently changed its currency from the mark to the euro.

Germany has one of the world's strongest **economies**. Many large companies have their main offices in Germany. The former East Germany, however, still needs a lot of help. A great deal of money is being spent to improve motorways and railways in the east. Germans are spending money to reduce noise and air pollution, too, and people are trying to protect the forests for the future.

Germans are proud of their country. When you leave Germany, people will say 'Auf Wiedersehen'. These are the German words that mean 'goodbye' in English.

You can visit Germany's parliament building, the Reichstag.

Quick facts about GERMANY

Capital
Berlin

Borders
Denmark, Netherlands, Belgium,
Luxembourg, France, Switzerland,
Austria, Czech Republic, Poland

Area
356,910 square kilometres
(137,803 square miles)

Population
83,029,536

Largest Cities
Berlin (3,458,763 people)
Hamburg (1,707,986 people)
Munich (1,225,809 people)
Cologne (964,346 people)
Frankfurt (647,304 people)

Main crops
grains, potatoes, sugar beet

Natural resources
coal, potash, lignite, iron, uranium

Major rivers
Elbe, Weser, Ems, Rhine and Main

28

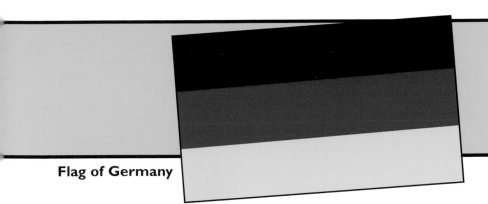

Flag of Germany

Coastline
2389 km (1493 miles)

Monetary unit
euro

Literacy rate
99 per cent

◀ **Major industries**
steel, ship-building, vehicles, machinery, coal, electronics, chemicals, iron, cement, food and drink

Glossary

Bavaria (Buh-VARE-ee-ah) largest state in Germany, located in the south of the country

Brandenburg Gate (BRAN-den-burg) gate that was built between 1788–1791 as an entrance to the city of Berlin

cathedral large church where an area's bishop is based

communism (KOM-mew-nism) political system where people work for and are taken care of by the state

democracy (deh-MOK-rah-see) political system where the rulers of a country are elected by the people

economy how a country controls and balances the value of money and the prices of goods and services

federal republic (FEH-deh-rahl reh-PUB-lik) when several states are joined together to form a country

industry making of goods and products

Munich (MEW-nik) capital of the Bavarian region and Germany's third largest city.

Muslim (MUHZ-lim) follower of Islam, the religion founded by the prophet Mohammed in the 7th century CE. Muslims believe in one God, Allah.

natural resources things from nature that are useful to people

parliament place where a country's elected officials meet to make laws

Protestant Christian churches that broke away from the Catholic Church in the 16th century

Reichstag (RIKE-stag) building that is the centre of Germany's government. Reichstag means parliament.

Rhine (RINE) longest river in western Europe. The Rhine winds through most of Germany, Switzerland and the Netherlands to the North Sea.

Roman Catholic Christian church, based in Rome, Italy, that considers the Pope to be Christ's representative on Earth

spa (SPAR) place that has natural springs where people bathe for health reasons

sauerkraut (SOUR-krout) German food made from fermented cabbage leaves

transport move something from one place to another

Index